The Splintered Face
Tsunami Poems

The Splintered Face
Tsunami Poems

Indran Amirthanayagam

Hanging Loose Press
Brooklyn, New York

Published by Hanging Loose Press, 231 Wyckoff Street, Brooklyn, New York 11217. All Rights Reserved. No part of this book may be reproduced without the publisher's written permission, except for brief quotations in reviews.

www.hangingloosepress.com

Printed in the United States of America
10 9 8 7 6 5 4 3 2 1

Hanging Loose thanks the Literature Program of the New York State Council on the Arts for a grant in support of the publication of this book.

Cover art by Greg Decker
Cover design by Marie Carter

Acknowledgments: Some of these poems appeared or are scheduled to be published (in the original English or in Spanish or French translations by David Ojeda, Laure Karcher and the author) in *Hanging Loose*; *Only The Sea Keeps*; *South Asian Review*; *Nethra* (Sri Lanka); *Milenio, Alforja* (Mexico); *Isla Negra* (Italy); EXIT (Canada), *Tamil Week* and these Internet sites: *geocities, artepoetica* and *breveespacio*. Some have also been set to music by Omar Tamez and presented by the author with the group Non-Jazz. The author wishes to thank Madelyn Miller for encouraging these poems and Dick Lourie for his careful eye and ear as their editor.

Library of Congress Cataloging-in-Publication Data

Amirthanayagam, Indran
  The splintered face : tsunami poems / Indran Amirthanayagam.
    p. cm.
  ISBN 978-1-931236-83-6 -- ISBN 978-1-931236-82-9 (pbk.)
  1. Tsunamis--Sri Lanka--Poetry. 2. Indian Ocean Tsunami, 2004--Poetry. I. Title. PR9440.9.A65S65 2008
    821'.914--dc22
                                                    2008043809

 Produced at The Print Center, Inc. 225 Varick St., New York, NY 10014, a non-profit facility for literary and arts-related publications. (212) 206-8465

Contents

III Eyewitness

IV Ghosts

For Anandan and Lola,
son and daughter, who bounce
on the belly of my heart,
who revive me each morning
with their questions.

For all the children of the tsunami,
survivors of the dice thrown
by human and god:
let that wave stay away
for more than a thousand years.

That Ceylon light gave me life,
gave me death at the same time,
because living inside a diamond
is a solitary lesson in being buried,
is like turning into a transparent bird,
a spider who spins the sky and says goodbye.

—from "That Light" by Pablo Neruda
(translated by Alastair Reid)

Preface

I find it hard to write even today about this tremendous beast, this roaring, yapping churn of water that scissored through the lives of more than 225,000 human beings on December 26th, 2004. The 35,000 washed away, or bludgeoned to death, in Sri Lanka, woke me up metaphorically in a sea bath although I was far away in Rockville, Maryland, at my mother's home. My father had not lived to see this freak attack on the island, which was engaged otherwise in its usual cat and mouse between rebels and government, although in 2004 the ceasefire held still and the islanders were in a festive mood.

It was the day after Christmas, Boxing Day, and they were sleepy-eyed, and unaware of the ominous signs, a sea receding revealing hundreds of fish gasping for air, brackish, angry water, and animals scurrying for higher ground, birds flying inland. On the Andaman Islands some people still close to birds and beasts picked up the signals and headed for safety. They were a drop literally in the sea's bucket. They are heroes of these poems even though they may never read them. But what about the men and women who went to peer at the sea bed? The ones who picked up huge fish and dashed for shore delighted at their luck? They too deserve a Boswell. They must all be written about, by writers "writing endlessly," as one of the poems observes. And then the wise elephants, the kingfishers and mynahs, snakes, lizards and monkeys? They knew the earth had turned wild, that we would all be thumped. They too are heroes of these poems.

My brother David wrote about the beached fish and bereft fishermen in his poem "Fishermen: Boxing Day 2004," where he says in part:

Wives and sons and lonely daughters
Are laid on human biers,

Wail in strange agony with no lesson,
Clamber through the bric-a-brac
Become prey for the fishers of men.

How do we find the cause of this
Strange upswelling, this sea surge?
The farmer caste and the mountain dwellers,
Darkling ponderers, would call them back
These fishermen, for questioning.

But they are gone, the way of graveyards,
Gone to flowers, an ocean bodily blooming . . .

His words reminded me that one can overcome the natural and shocked silence that results from tragedy. When my father died I started to write about his life on the plane as I flew to my parents' home in Rockville. Now on the day my country of birth lost half its face, I needed to write that face back. I hope these poems made in the urgent hours, days and weeks after December 26th—with the distance now of time and the sad accumulation of other disasters—will help the reader remember, bear witness, pray, kiss the beloved, run outside and shout to the birds and flowers we are alive and we are grateful for the borrowed day, the extra time.

My father, Guy Amirthanayagam, left us while waiting to receive communion at the church up the road, a stone's throw from the garden he cultivated with my mother, these awesome colors, the inevitable unplanned flowers.

I
The Unplanned Flower

The Unplanned Flower

In my lusty garden there are bougainvilleas
Red, white and mauve: even temperate azaleas
Purpling among the green, recusant roses
Toned down to tropical colour, poses
Of unclimatic bravado; all my hard affection
Revels in corybantic profusion.

I am ambitious: I want my stamp
On these my efforts, though the climate is forbidding.
An arrogant florescence of my lamp
Pitted against the wind, and nature's slow dying.

But what issues from my daimon and my art,
And dredges the symbol of all my endeavour
Is this unwilled, demonic flower
With flaming yellow petals, and a black heart.

—Guy Amirthanayagam

Face

Imagine half your face
rubbed out yet
you are suited up
and walking
to the office.

How will your mates
greet you?
with heavy hearts,
flowers,
rosary beads?

How shall we greet
the orphan boy,
the husband whose hand
slipped, children
and wife swept away?

How to greet
our new years
and our birthdays?
Shall we always
light a candle?

Do we remember
that time erases
the shore, grass
grows, pain's
modified?

At Hikkaduwa
in 1980 I wrote a ditty,
a sailor's song
about rain
in sunny Ceylon.

I don't know
what Calypsonians
would compose
about this monstrous
wave, this blind hatchet man;

don't know
the Baila singers' reply;
we are a "happy and
go" people
yet the fisherman's wife

knows
that her grandfather
was eaten by the ocean—
fisher communities
have suffered in time

and what's happened
now is just another feast
for that bloody,
sleeping mother
lapping at our island;

but what if the ocean
were innocent,
the tectonic plates
innocent, what if God
were innocent?

                *

I do not know
how to walk upon the beach,
how to lift corpse
after corpse
until I am exhausted,

how to stop the tears
when half my face
has been rubbed out
beyond
the railroad tracks

and this anaesthetic,
this calypso come
to the last verse.
What shall we write
in the sand?

Where are gravestones
incinerated? Whose
ashes are these urned
and floating through a house
throttled by water?

Shall we build
a memorial
some calculated distance
from the sea, in a park,
in the shape of a giant wave

where we can write
the names of the dead?
Has the wave lost
its beauty? Is it now
considered obscene?

*

Yet tomorrow
we must go to the ocean
and refresh ourselves
in the sea breeze
down in Hikkaduwa

where it is raining
in sunny Ceylon.
Tomorrow, we must
renew our vows
at sunrise, at sunset.

Let us say the next time
the ocean recedes
and parrots gawk
and flee, and restless
dogs insist their humans

wake up, we will not peer
at the revelation
of the ocean bed,
nor seek photographs.
We will run to higher ground,

and gathered there
with our children,
our cats, dogs,
pigs, with what we've
carried in our hands

—albums, letters—
we will make a circle,
kneel, sit,
stand in no particular
direction, pray

and be silent,
open our lungs
and shout thanks
to our gods
thanks to our dogs.

Commandment

Trincomalee,
      Batticaloa,
succulent baths
     in sea pools

for the odd jellyfish,
wading waist-deep for miles
on my father's shoulders
this inheritance I carry;

now names return
where the sea drew back
exposing rocks
huge like elephants,

then catapulted,
bludgeoning beaches,
bodies roused out
of seething, headless water,

The five-hundred-mile-an-hour
funeral march;
how to recover the poise
of the emerald?

"The sea is coming,"
a fisher boy shouted.
"Thou shalt
not," I replied.

The Last Picture

Imagine
a ninety-year-old painter,
strong, body
like a leather stick,

skin burnt
from so many suns
and walks
along the beach,

a natural
philosopher, virile,
inspiration
for his grandchildren

who play in the pools
watching small fish
the last wave
brought in.

Imagine, a holiday,
a full moon,
the family
back at home,

and he finishes
his still life:
a giant wave,
agitated, dirty,

the waiting sand.

Century

That horrific speed:
five-hundred-mile-
an-hour knife
hurtling towards
our island
to gash and gut
the coast, unearth
childhood treasures
and landmines,

popped out
for public display
in the silt and mud,
the tsunami's
gift and curse,
psychotherapy
instant and forced
for you the survivor
who lives on

the other side
of the sea. You've
got memories
back now, and
a morning: write
the dirge,
from beginning
to community's
end, yet build

your house
again brick
by brick, savoring
each metaphor
like the first time
you knocked
a century at Lord's
and the crowd
stood up in praise.

Interpretation

Mass
at Our Lady
of Matara

was
interrupted
that Sunday
morning,

her doors
flung
open
to greet

the
prodigal
son.

A Question of Trains

Cheran writes, from the beach
in Bentota with his sister
and her children on Boxing Day,
they saw the furious sea
and began to run
ahead of the first wave,
up the hotel stairs
to their third floor room
just in time. The wave knocked

out the first floor, returned
for the second. The staircase stood.
Cheran and family for twenty
minutes stood, then waded
through the receding flood
to the highest ground,
Bentota Railway Station,
which by some miracle
was still sending off trains.

By the time the third wave hit,
they were on their way back
to Colombo, while further south
the *Queen of the Sea,* the famous
honeymooners' train, bludgeoned
off the tracks at Peraliya, left
passengers—and villagers who climbed
aboard trying to escape the rising waters—
almost 2,000 people, dead.

Words and Orchids

We had gone for a sea bath
and had just sat down to eat
mangos and *pittu,* a spicy
poll sambol. My husband
was thrilled with home food
and sea air, the orchids
the waiter arranged
elaborately
on our table. I wanted
the flowers moved

because they blocked
my view of the sea,
but my husband insisted.
He said the waiter had
taken such trouble
and in the States
how often would we eat
mangos by an ocean
framed with orchids.
Those were his last words.

When the first wave roared
over us, I held on to a palm tree,
then as the water receded
ran and ran uphill. Met
our friends there but
my husband stayed behind.
I do not have his body,
just these words about flowers,
his grin as he sucked
mangos with his hands.

Train

On the morning
of the last day
the passengers
climbed aboard
the *Queen of the Sea*,

laden with gifts,
entwined, speaking
on the train
of their holiday
to be.

They rode
with glee
(unaware)
smashed now
into history.

Global Village

We
stood
between
lagoon
and sea.

We live
in a glosbal
village;
had been
watching

cricket
from New
Zealand
that morning.
Why couldn't

somebody
warn us?
The minister
says
it was Poya Day,

a holiday:
Nobody saw
the message
from Hawaii..
What rubbish.

If we had known,
we could have
taken our wives
and children
on our boats

into the middle
of the lagoon.
They are
offering
30,000 rupees

to build
here again.
What rubbish.
You see
that tree,

that high high
tree, that's where
my aunt held
on and she
lived; my son . . .

King Kong

King Kong was four years old
and trying already to lift weights
like his father Chinnathambi,
the bodybuilder, when the waves
washed him away
with his brothers and mother.
Now, Chinnathambi sits
like an orphan beside his house
broken to the foundation stones.

In Amy Waldman's report
he returns every day
to Navalady, to the scene
of the crime, to guard
what's left of his belongings
and vow that he will come
back to stay, but then
within an hour or a day,
he is less certain

that he could live
again with that water
boiling in the morning—
"wife and mother-in-law
holding on to my neck,
I tried to swim then hit a wall
and when I woke up
I saw a naked woman
and swam to find my family"—

And does he think:
Who will say Dada now?
Who will care for me
when I grow old and cannot
lift a woman with my leg,
or 330 pounds of cement?
My sons and wife
must have thought
my strength would save them;

they must now eat
at this 30-day feast,
oil lamps are lit
and the banana leaves
full of sweetmeats:
tell me your wishes,
my family, show me
the way back here, or
take me with you.

Belt

Instructions say
to secure
your belt
and jacket
before
tucking
in your child.

When the wave
struck, my son
held me tight,
his fingers
pressed
in my
shoulders;

water
engulfed us,
I panicked
thinking
we would
drown; I
let him go

thinking
he would
have a better
chance
to survive.
I lived.
He died.

Bill

Daughter dawdled in bed
that morning. I packed bags,
put petrol in the car, then
we went up to eat. That hotel's
designed in a spiral, and
breakfast was served
at the top. "Something strange

is happening to the sea," a man
shouted. "We are going to die."
I rushed to the window,
the whole bay had emptied
and shoals of huge fish
were flapping and gasping
on the bed. Herds of people

could not believe the sight
and ran to the sea, tried
to grab fish, drag them
to shore. Then I looked up
and saw the wave. I turned.
Wife and daughter had gone.
Chaos. I kept thinking about

the car, ready for our journey
back to Colombo. No lights.
No power. Computers out.
I stood at reception trying
to pay. Wife and daughter
found me. I felt terrible
to leave without paying my bill.

Birds

Birds that eat salt,
hang about cemeteries,
forage in abandoned lots,
civil war crows
fattened on carnage
from roadside bombs,
gorged vultures
loping from body
to body, picking
eyes clean
before clambering
up into trees
that have survived
hanging still
over the silent
beach.

II
Silence

Silence

Bodies float in my silence,
trees are uprooted, waves
masticate timber, split
roof beams, in my silence,

babies tossed into palm
fronds, old man alone
on a beach engulfed
by seething mobs of foam

and spray, in my silence,
moments of clairvoyance
seeing whole populations
of islands and coastal wetlands,

inlets and lagoons, splits
and wedges of sandbars
and sandy points, convulsed
by churning of dirty grey

water, this starfish-laden
fish-spouting sea
turning blue again slowly,
in my silence.

Waiter

Iresh saved three fat women
from beyond the ramparts
at Galle Fort. He lumbered
up the stone steps, almost
fell. Back in his village

at Weligame: father
sailed away, mother
and sister clambered
up a tree. Aunty drowned,
lots of children perished.

"The other day was
Aunty's alms-giving, end
of this week my father's.
The three women came
back from their home

in Ambalangoda, found
the hotel owner and gave
him thanks. Not one word
to me. Sri Lanka,
You know how we are."

Salt

The nutritionist
    walks
in the wasteland
with her translators
from plot to plot.

Four houses stood
there, Madam;
all the wells
are salty, the palm
trees will die.

That house, yes,
resisted the blast,
but its owners,
the sea
moved them out.

Lead

I couldn't believe my luck,
the biggest story of my life
yet this saddest catastrophe:
background of palm trees,
whistling death, bodies
stacked on the beach;

clambering through
bric-a-brac
of a once elegant hotel,
umbrellas, mortar,
ceiling fans blown
into the swimming pool,

owner pointing
to the remains
of a room
where a wheel-
chaired man
embraced his wife.

We do not know
what they said;
we lost nine here
but will rebuild. This
hotel has withstood
civil war, entertained

visitors in tails and
evening gowns
before World War Two—
ah, Ceylon escaped
that calamity, except
for the whistling

of Japanese bombers
and rationing, lack
of soap and clothes,
breakdown of transport.
Now, we have
Boxing Day,

Thumped
on Boxing Day,
Washed Away
On Boxing Day,
Buried
on Boxing Day.

How will you lead,
man, about
the will to rebuild?
historic shock?
disabled man
clasping his wife?

Green Sea

Sea green, not blue,
bed full of sand,
flotsam, bodies,
waves still
unsettled,

twenty-foot-high
breakers
make fun
of the makeshift
matted boat

setting out
for the first time
since December 26th,
hungry family
waiting for the catch,

no other way
but face the waves
again, yet questions
persist about moves
to the city

or the mountains,
images of green
fields, beetroot, bulbs,
milking cows mixed
with furious swells

in daydreams and
nightmares, yet
the sea is father
and mother,
karma and dharma

and all other
available terms,
including fate,
that explain
why waves killed

twenty-five members of
my neighbor's family
but spared me
to see
this sea green.

Lovers

Lovers have returned
to Galle Face Green
"under quivering
umbrellas,"
says the report,
in bushes,
by rocks
at the sea's edge . . .

but not
on the East Coast
where debris
smells still
and palm trees
bend laden
with salt.
For how long

shall we hold
hands, cuddle,
exchange
love words
on evening walks
by our private beaches.
When may we return
to the East Coast?

Baby 81 in New York

Baby 81 pulled out
of the mud, united
with his parents
after DNA tests

in Colombo, invited
to New York by
*Good Morning,
America.*

My friend writes
the boy's beautiful,
gladdened
the Big Apple.

The other eight
mothers who claimed
the child, if they can
still be found,

will receive
consolation prizes
from the station: coffee
mugs, posters, this poem.

Beads and Whiskey

A joyful and sorrowful mystery:
this baby, a few weeks old,
found in an alcove under
loads of bric-a-brac and mud,
while the chainsaw
scissored the houses all round,

a child claimed by nine
mothers, subject of Solomon,
DNA tests, in the end
one set of parents insisted
and traveled to Colombo
for the procedure; the others

adjusted themselves to destiny,
to rosary beads and coconut whiskey.

Teaching Noah

When Noah built his ark, all the species crawled, walked, hopped, flew on board without a second thought. They were offered free passage, fodder and a window. The closeness of serpent, tarantula and microbe to clean beasts and Shem, Ham and Japheth and their wives and children did not bother Noah, or the writers of the history. These clean and unclean beasts and humans lived together for one hundred and fifty days while the waters filled the earth, and for several months more while the waters receded and ravens and doves went out to look for dry land.

Incredible, like loaves and fishess later on in the story of the carpenter, this ark made of gopher, three hundred cubits long, fifty wide, thirty high—and to end up on top of a mountain with all that precious cargo, the very substance of life, and the kicking hungers of clean and unclean beasts wanting to get a bit of leg and thigh and multiply, keeping the fevers in check until Noah extracts the olive branch out of the teeth of a dove and says yes the waters have dried and we can return to our homes, rebuild them with brick and mortar, and even beside the sea.

Stuck

The clock's
arms
at the Harbor
Master's office
in Galle froze
at 9:27 a.m.

      *

An Indian
Navy patrol
received
urgent orders
to rush
to the island

but could
not enter
port
for floating
bodies and
broken boats.

      *

Facing No Man's
Land officials,
full of cash,
lorries laden
with supplies,
have a conundrum:
distribute or divert?

Intruder: Mullaitivu

I felt
like an intruder
in that house.

The Christmas
presents
were still wrapped,

the statue
of Christ
dried out.

Rescue: Galle

Broken coconut tree
flotsam
    on the beach,

children
    of the tsunami
come back

to salvage
    from the wreck
beside

a huge
dumpster
    brought by sea

and four hundred
    Marines
        clearing debris.

Reprieved

Kadalaxshiaman
who guards the sea
washed out of her temple
and flung 110 yards
inland at Navalady,

Our Lady, 400 years
of encrusted gold, swept
from her Matara church,
salvaged after the tsunami
from a nearby garden—

deities restored
now to their altars,
with garlands
of fresh white petals,
their helplessness

before the monstrous
waves forgiven and
forgotten: a miracle
to have been dislodged
but not destroyed,

their faith reprieved.

Faith

Every morning
I raise the host,
see my congregation,
and beyond
the doors the ocean.

We lost eighteen nuns
that day, and the old,
venerated statue
of the Virgin washed up
in a nearby garden.

We have cleaned
the church. God's
will is beyond
our understanding.
There was nothing

more beautiful
in the morning
than the lapping
of waves and the cries
of seabirds,

a natural chorus
to our human voices.
We have prayed
for the sisters
and parishioners

swept away.
We are saying
Mass again,
doors wide open
to raucous gulls,

calm ocean.
We cannot
toss out our church.
God did not move
the foundation.

III
Eyewitness

Eyewitness

She's an angry bugger,
sleeping monster,
murderer; look
at how our people
suffer, coast devoured,
reef diced up
when the waves
roared through,

blind, brutal, blood-
thirsty, but she is
our mother;
we are islanders;
she has fed,
circled,
brooded us,
let our boats

come and go,
and monkeys build
a bridge for Rama
to bring Sita back.
Give us our bodies
now and be off
to sleep. We remain
your children

after the flood,
and come with new
bricks and mortar
to ask for your blessing.
We don't want
to leave you alone,
build far from shore.
You are our mother.

We'll not abandon
you in the madhouse,
commit you
to the hospice.
Give us your fish
again, your fragility
in coral,
free passage.

Boy

Hospital bed,
Bangalore,
a boy recovers
from his wounds,
cared for now
by doctors
and his uncle.

From time
to time,
he dials
his parents'
cell number,
says he'll heal
then return

to Yala,
ask the
elephants
and birds
to find
Appa and
Amma.

Cycle

They lived
on coconut water
for 38 days—

unnoticed
in the scrambling
of Man trying

to repair himself
elsewhere, limbs
wedged in trees,

pulled out
of boats beached
on the high street—

nine men, women
and children
smiling, found

on the southern
tip of the
Andaman Isles

miraculous,
leftover news
inserted into

the second month
of the tsunami cycle,
devoted otherwise

now to stories
of renewal, picking
up stones to rebuild

houses, make
amends with the sea,
get back to work.

Tower (Ark)

During the night's rain
and broken sleep
I climbed
the lookout;

dreamt
of a fortress
on a peak,
Sigiriya,

with a picture
window
of reinforced
glass,

and down below
a furious wave,
a beach and
the mouths of babies

crying—I turned
in my turret
of sound mind,
sound body

too high
and far away
to break
the glass

but for writing
I found plenty
floating
in the ark.

Runner

A long distance runner
paces his race,
does not exhaust himself
in a frantic flash
at the start, just to say

that once he led
the Olympic Marathon
for five miles
or even five yards.
At Munich in '72

I remember rooting
for the Sri Lankan
who sped past
the pack early on.
I wonder what's become

of that island hero
now that all the heroes
have come back
to pick up the fallen
stones, to unsalt the wells.

Has he spent his energy
on the first set of flotsam?
Perhaps he's an accountant
or clerk, some cog in an office,
and the waves have allowed

him to shine, to walk
his hands down to the beach,
to clean up the bric-a-brac
of what was once his home,
find an old snapshot among

the fallen planks: a young
man beaming framed
by two *frauleins* holding
tankards of frothy ale:
Munich the night before the race.

Fish

I walk the beach
dressed in a shroud,
on a secret visit
to speak only
with souls
at sea, to ask
how their bodies
have decomposed,
if they'd now
approve
our casting nets,
eating fish.

The fishermen
who survived
have begun repairs
on their broken boats,
salvaged wrecks
from trees and streets.
The price of fish
has doubled, while
the number of buyers
has dwindled to a handful
of curious strangers,
visitors, exotics.

Rain

Cold twist of rain
penetrates skin; thought
washed, dreamed,
trapped in sheets, I break

through waters shaking
off sleep to greet streaked
windowpanes
and a hummingbird

crashing glass,
leaving tiny, wet prints.
How shall I drink
this rain . . . my island

friends tumbling
out into ocean,
trying to latch
on to trees

also uprooted
and flung back to a beach
filled with the rubbish
of a city smithereened?

Speed

Government promised
50,000 new houses
in Hambantota
where the lagoon's
been drained
of hundreds of bodies
and the homeless
have become
loud in their misery

cursing and stamping
their feet when
the minister laid
foundation stones
for the first residence—
some sixty days
after the tsunami
spurred its planners
into a frenzy.

Exercise

Dress smart,
hook your dog up
and walk to the park
after drinking
green tea,

a morning ablution,
the walk brisk,
on your mind
a gigantic wave,
hungry, dark birds

of prey, but
the walk will dice
the birds up
like balls of fat,
and going

to the train
station will mean
just a ride, not
the self deposited
on the tracks.

I...Was Here

The conductor
has returned,
after a month,
to the field

where the wave
heaved his train
from the tracks.
He's brought

his two children
and wife
who find bits
of his uniform

in the rubbish.
1,500 people
died on the train.
He'll preserve

the uniform.
Further along
the tracks,
in his home

village, a husband
and wife separate
useful bricks
one by one

from the dust heap,
to rebuild
their house
brick by brick.

In another village
by the tracks,
a reporter spots
a solitary tent

and a man
painting his name
and address
on its canvas.

Bosched

They appear to me
like souls
in Purgatory
hanging
from rafters, palms,
overturned hulls,
floating cars,
while waves
return after
spattering dirty
grey seed
over beaches
and bedrooms,
flower gardens,
schools,
orphanages—
the city, *machan*,
like a virgin delivered
to her husband
on the wedding day.

Transport

Fishermen have always
sewn palm fronds
and thatched homes
a stone's throw from the ocean,
dragging the family's portion
of the catch right to their doors.

These quadrangles erected
in planners' books,
miles from the sea,
do not smell of salt or fish,
or swing in the breeze—they mock
impermanence with cement . . .

and require fishermen
to take buses or three-wheelers
to their workplaces, pick up
boats from the communal parking
lot, set off to fish,
perturbed, with yet further to go

when they get back to shore.

Somebody's Aunt

I remember a tale
in *Running in the Family*
about an aunt washed away
by a monsoon.

A family can digest
the loss of an aunt,
fill the tableau
with a wink at death

and go on with the party;
not *this* time,
not for whole clans
and neighborhoods

drowned in a flash,
yet the aunt flooded
in a rocking chair,
sporting a red bandanna,

(Ondaatje's relative,
read thirty years ago,
dressed
by my imagination)

hollers still
down the avenue
in my kaleidoscope
mixed

with red eggs
hatched
in Granny's coop,
jellyfish

snapping
my ankles
in Trincomalee
before I screamed

and my father
scooped me up;
kaleidoscope
fractures, shards:

cricket bat, comb,
on Rest House Road
every house returned
to foundation stone,

the well still moored,
brackish now,
stuffed with wood,
a body, somebody's aunt.

Plumb Line

There are hundreds of bodies
in the lagoon at Hambantota;
I wonder about the salt flats,
commissioner's bungalow,
thick, green forest
where monkey troupes
would gather in force
before swooping down
to the verandah
for sugar bowls.

I think about the carom
table's zinging discs
fixed in my childhood,
transistor radios
broadcasting songs of Ceylon,
chat about latest novels
and poems from London,
our sense then of being tied
to the center of a language far away
via the miracle of transmitters.

Transmissions now are somber,
reports from ruins
of an innocence lost already
in war's butchery, Man's
inhumanity, these truths we ignore
unearthed like landmines
as we move on muttering
muttering through international
conferences, forgiveness of debt,
how easy, we shall do what's possible,

the rest is for memory,
laments, forgetfulness,
carom table waterlogged,
bungalow broken up,
lagoon smelling and heavy,
cursed with human bodies:
who will eat fish now?
Which generation will play
here unaware? Shall we forget
by decree? by forgiveness?

Will our gods,
our governments,
our seismic indicators,
reveal an answer?

IV
Ghosts

Ghosts

The ghosts will need food,
bed sheets, towels,
birthdays celebrated,
children washed, clothed.

They will require white
candles, low-cut wicks,
nothing ostentatious,
a small altar, table

in the living room,
in a corner, to keep
an eye on the children
as they study and dream,

put flesh on their arms,
become young men
and women, get drunk,
fall in love.

The ghosts will
not leave us
to grow up
unattached, alone.

Arithmetic

Muthiah
likes arithmetic,
keeps his mind fit.

He's 70 and
gathering palm fronds
on the beach,

about to rebuild
only 300 yards
from the water's edge.

He says a tsunami
comes every
100 years.

He will
count
out his days.

Surviving Houses

Word's out
that houses of worship—
churches, temples, mosques—
survived the blast; yes
icons were dislodged,
shoved up the road,
but have been put back
and the ceremonies
of innocence begun,
a new season,

horticulturalists
in high demand, snap-
dragons, irises, flame-
of-the-forest,
ubiquitous
plumerias, barrels
full of flowers picked
in the gardens
of Nuwara Eliya,
rattling down

the slopes to festoon
newly scrubbed
and chastened houses
who saw priests
and nuns washed away,
flocks decimated,
but have made amends,
found strength
and innocence
(and their statues) again.

Pooja

I scoured the newspapers
and Web this morning
but did not find the 76th day
anniversary of the tsunami
cited. Difficult to keep
daily *pooja*, cut
jasmine flowers
and break coconuts
at the temple doors.

In these mountains,
coconuts are a specialty
item at the HEB, and
Catholic churches
do not encourage
heaping servings
of rice, plantains
and yogurt at the feet
of their images.

If I could take India
into my hands like
a ball of rice and curry
and eat in front
of everybody, pierce
the billion names
of god into one god
ring rattling
from my nose

that would make
my neighbors swoon
and me feel at home
in the silence of canyons,
church naves open
only on feast days,
Sundays, where the ablution
of holy water has been
removed for questions of hygiene.

Writers

"They have come and written,
written and gone,
everybody's writing endlessly,"
Maheshwaran said of officials
with tall ledgers and fountain pens,
details of people and goods lost
making order on paper, filling
filing cabinets in nearby Batticaloa

City, the town of Navalady
documented: 500 rupees paid
to new bachelors, 1,000
to ones who managed to keep
a spouse alive, refugees now
at Methodist Central College
soon to move to a new tent city,
afraid of the sea, howling at night

in the classrooms; Chinnathambi
Selvam, bodybuilder, "who could eat
10 and a half loaves of bread at a sitting,
lift a woman with one leg, hoist
330 pounds of cement" but could not
save his four sons or wife—written
by Amy Waldman in the *New York
Times*—everybody writing endlessly.

Thirty days after the tsunami,
survivors haul giant banana leaves
on boats, riding to Navalady,
a spit of land between sea and lagoon—
Southern administration
and Wanni, where the Tigers rule—
to peel onions, fry yams and fish,
feed their dead as is custom,

sit by oil lamps and candles,
in some cases burn stumps
of palmyra trees, and assure
the ghosts will eat,
wishes met, and this writing
flicker like lanterns
in the sea breeze, at night,
making metaphors with the dead.

School

Girl hesitates
at the door,
single pigtail
in the lintel's shade.

I do not know
whom she has lost.
Alone
in the half-light,

bright sun
beyond
in the playground,
she steps back,
forward, back.

I walk with
the camera past
stumps of desks
and drying school

records. Girl
walks through
the door. Boy,
eyes wide open,

only child now
of his grandmother,
their fingers clasped,
waits in line

before a teacher
who writes down
names of those
left in their family,

who says a new class
will form
so another girl she knows
will have company,

this boy, that girl
walking now through
the playground, single
pigtail, eyes wide wide.

On Holiday, By Another Sea

Mix greens and slice almonds,
baste sun-ripened tomatoes
with olive oil, add sprigs of basil,
this Mediterranean feast

in a room by the sea at Nice,
Persian windows, striped chairs,
an afternoon Matisse, delicate,
caressing breezes, odalisque

on the divan, yet the picture
does not satisfy; the renter
has brought his own pestilence
to the scene, boiling flies

and gangrene, black-blooded
sea full of trees and cars,
aluminium sheets, bodies
barreling down the street . . .

if he could shut off the spout . . .
make the world dry, absorb
breezes and courtesan's kisses,
take large gulps of wine.

Wrecked: Coconuts

I lost all my companions,
walked from village
to village, found a large knife,
husked coconuts and ate
until a ship found me,
25 days later they said,
on the beach,
emaciated but alive.

I want to go back.
There is no other
life for me
but casting nets.
My wife and children
were swept away,
but I will find
myself company.

Would anybody
like to join me back
on the island?
I will plant a garden.
There are coconuts
and fish. The sea
is gentle
most of the time.

Elephants

I think of the elephants
who gave rides to children,
lifted them up with their trunks
and carried them to higher ground,

tuskers, lifting roof beams
and cement markers,
clearing rubbish
after the waves retired—

what reward
do they deserve?
One hundred acres of pure
second growth forest,

certified, that will not
be tilled or cut?
How about liberation
on the city streets,

a weekend pass?
I suggest we trust
that nobody
will be trampled,

that we've taken
the necessary
precautions
to let our fellow animals

roam freely among us.
Let's put these
elephants on a stage:
marvels, heroes among men.

History: Mullaitivu

These were houses,
a playground,
church.

Those foundation
stones belonged
to the orphanage

for children
of the war. Even
the palm trees

are poisoned,
the winds howl
with ghosts,

the sun wakes
up bloody,
the night's

a cold moon.
Let us away
inland to dig

new wells.
In time
archaeologists

will dig up
evidence
of these human

settlements.

Order

Jesus did not ride that monstrous wave,
not Yahweh, Jah, Allah, none of the major

Gods or the minor ones, not even the godless
strode that bugger which sliced our lives

in two: the past where we danced ballroom
while the children played carom, and mangos

stained our lapels, and today, hobbling,
scavenging in ash heaps, how easy

the arithmetic, day and night, two by two.
Bring on the mind workers.

Let a thousand doctors bloom.
I lived right here on the x, my name

is blue: sea green blue blue green
I do not speak in tongues. I am not

disordered, a babbler. I did not lose
anybody close to me, just 30,000

fellow island bees, not to worry, *machan*,
old fellow, I will subscribe tomorrow,

the order of every day, skip and jump rope,
whistle, talk to aid workers, even swim.

Girl Dressed

I will not forget
the girl in her Sunday dress
playing on the beach

two weeks now
after the waves razed
her house and neighborhood

but spared her and the dress
and countless other children
who will pick up seashells,

make kites from palm fronds,
hit cricket balls,
get back then to their games

and fabled innocence,
even though before the waves
civil war finished off

innocence early, sent
generations abroad
to new playing fields,

to adjust themselves
to the pleasure
and bitterness

of a nostalgia
that recalls waves
rising and breaking

shifting sands
by fisher huts, thatched
with fronds, a useless,

sweet nostalgia
for the world
before the flood

where a girl played
on the beach,
who plays still

and the flood's
a metaphor in a book
of ethics and faith—

now this modern
deluge will be
chronicled

for a girl who'll
grow tall and study,
go abroad

and recall waves,
distant and foreboding,
and her dress on a Sunday.

Borders

Let's not speak
of countries or homelands;
there's an ocean
and beach
full of bodies,
and a sea unaware

of human calamity,
moon bright
in some lover's eye,
sparrows
the morning after
returned to dance.

Let's pick up
the dead now, all
the peace agreements,
insurance papers.
Let's walk across
the borders now.

Come Together

I watch the scene
via satellite: tents,
latrine, powdered milk,
rice and dhal,
nurse and mobile

clinic, inevitable
and welcome ordering,
visit of DDT sprayers,
even the odd smile
of relief, children

playing with timber
bits, bat salvaged
from a ruined house,
my doctor cousin
on his way to Pottuvil

from Brooklyn,
suitcase full of ointments;
engineer from town
unversed in wells
helps anyway to drain the salt,

friend in Manhattan
brings writers together
to read poems about water,
throughout the planet
memory acts:

kids bake cookies,
star in ads for
Save the Children,
the tsunami generation
between mountain and sea,

on street corners in Torreon
and San Luis, jangling cups
for *Caritas*: two pesos
per car at the stoplights,
auctions and star-

splashed telethons, we have
come together for a time:
hands on the ground
cleaning wounds and coast,
hearts attached via satellite.

Some of the proceeds of the book will be donated to tsunami relief.